AF226281

# IF NOTHING ELSE...

## A COLLECTION OF POETRY WRITTEN IN 20 MINUTES OR LESS

THE SINGING PONY
PUBLISHING

First published in Canada in 2023 by
The Singing Pony Publishing

www.caklugofficial.com

ISBN: 978-1-7388466-1-0



A CIP catalogue record for this book is available from Library and Archives Canada.

*"During the height of the coronavirus pandemic, I did a lot of deep thinking. It's funny what sorts of things enter your mind at a time when so much uncertainty is rampant. At times, my thoughts and feelings became overwhelming, like a broken dam. So, I did what writers do: I wrote. My fears, my hopes, my opinions, my likes and dislikes—all of it. I wanted to capture these thoughts and feelings in their rawest, most poetic form, so I set a timer for 20 minutes before I picked up my pen. (Most of the time, I only needed 5-10 minutes.) Within these pages are my pure, unedited thoughts and feelings about the world and society, life and love, and above all, my everlasting desire for world peace. Not much order, but oddly, not much disorder either. I'm not out to boggle your mind, reader. I just hope that my words resonate kindly with you. That's all.*

*Stay well, and always be good."*

*— C.A.*

<u>2020—a world changed</u>

We've crashed.
Crashed to a halt.
We didn't want this;
we didn't ask for it.
But we have it.
There's no point asking why
or wishing it were different.
Those are only ways
to put off dealing with it.
And the longer we put it off,
the longer we'll remain
crashed.

<u>If nothing else</u>

If nothing else,
when I'm gone,
I want to be a good memory.
I want to be a smile,
and a laugh,
and an affectionate eyeroll.
If I can be those things,
I can still give peace
when I'm at peace.

Twenty minutes
is all it takes
for most things to run their course.
The joy from good news,
the pain from bad news,
the sorrow from loss,
the ache from fear,
the warmth from love...
Twenty minutes,
and they disappear.
What remains
and what you feel,
is simply a memory.
There's nothing left to see,
nothing left to hear,
nothing left to do.
So, we start to think.
And we immortalize those twenty short minutes
forever.

There is a perch, deep within my heart
where a little bird sits and sings.
Whistling, whistling, relentless and true.
No rest, no cares.
It has a job to do.
It knows me better than I know myself
because it listens to me.
With each whistle of its throat,
each flap of its wings,
My thoughts, my hopes, my dreams, it sings.
It is my message.
It is the philosopher when I am young,
and the cherub when I am old.
It is everything I am not, and yet
everything I am.
And so, I encourage this little bird to sing
and to flap its wings,
carrying my message near and far.
All day and all night, it sings and it flaps.
Do you hear it?

<u>What would happen?</u>


What would happen
if for once,
we all just listened?
Listened to the profound thoughts of children.
They are the future.
A future of hope and love,
but only if we listen.

What would happen
if for once,
we all just watched?
Watched as the seasons change outside.
The green fades to orange, and then to white,
guiding us through our own changes.
And how do we repay our Mother Earth?

What would happen
if for once,
we all just felt?
Felt with our hearts as naturally as we do with our hands.
Our hearts can feel far more
than we even know.
But only if we let them.

<u>The trees</u>

Sometimes I tell my troubles to the trees
because they don't judge me.
They listen, they consider, but make no reply
of course, because they are trees.
If I whisper my worries to the willows,
I will find the freedom I sought.
The weight those waving branches can hold,
My own shoulders cannot.
Firs can fathom my fears
because they have been afraid.
They are victims in this game called life,
which all of us humans have played.
I can entrust my energy to the elms.
I know they will not deplete me.
They give me air, space, and refuge,
and they do it for no fee.
And when I ponder my problems with the pines
I know I am not alone.
They release me of my burdens
just like they release their cones.
So, I tell my troubles to the trees
and let I them go on giving.
But I never forget how lucky I am
that they let me go on living.

There is a place
quite near to the heart.
It holds your lifetime, your memories,
and never tears them apart.
From the time that you are there
to the time that you are gone,
the beauty of this sacred place
will forever sing your song.
It is always there and waiting for you.
No matter how far you may roam,
there is absolutely no place
like your home.

<u>Kindness, part I</u>

To be kind
is to show your light.
And in a world
full of so much darkness,
isn't it always better
to shine bright?

<u>At the end of the day</u>

We all say 'at the end of the day'
as if the things that happen before the end
aren't important.
How come the end is what we focus on?
Why, when we get to the end,
do we forget the journey?

For those of you still in,
and those of you already out,
and those of you who aren't sure
what you're all about.
It's okay.
For those of you who don't need
to come out or stay in,
but still think love is beautiful,
and in no way a sin.
Thank you.
It's not our similarities
that give us our beauty.
We contribute our differences,
as is our duty.
The choice is yours.
To come out or stay in,
or to keep pondering the thought.
I do hope we'll support each other
because in the end, we're all we've got.

<u>Division</u>

What I don't understand
about division
is that it's brought on by difference.
If we could only see
that in each of our hearts lies a gift
to better the world,
something unique to ourselves
that no one else can give,
we wouldn't condemn difference.
We'd celebrate it.

I can't help but wonder
when things become bleak,
why activity is all that we seek.
Our minds
and more importantly,
our hearts
need time.
Time alone
to grieve,
to heal,
to adjust.
We need time,
but even if we have it,
we keep busy
rather than use it.
And I think
that we all think
ignoring the bleakness
is much less frightening
than taking the time
to deal with it.

The snowy winds roar past
as we look out at the darkness of our earth.
During this season,
cold as the ice it creates,

we wait for it all to melt away
as the rising sun appears again.
The green comes back,
the world is wet,

and it brings the flowers.
The sun is alive,
and the bees buzz happily as they search
the reds and purples for a sweet something.

When the bees go away and the green turns orange,
chills arrive and the sun goes back to sleep.
We adore the crunchy leaves floating freely
as the cycle begins again.

It's happy.
It's bright.
An array of green
fills the world
and reminds us
to be good.
Be good to our earth,
and be good to each other.
We sit at the window,
watching raindrops race,
longing to romp and play
under the golden warmth.
But the race is necessary
for the warmth
to be.
How good the earth is to us
is how good we must be in return.
After all,
a plentiful summer
can only come
from goodness.

My favourite colour is the leaves.
My favourite smell is the air.
Grey skies that don't threaten
render me without cares.
Say what you will about the trends:
the plaid, and the pumpkin spice.
To me, they are comfort,
and you know what? It's nice.
Veiled with shadow and spook,
perhaps it's not what we all seek.
But me, I wish it lasted longer
than just a few short weeks.
Embrace the grey and the cold to see
the beauty in each leaf that turns.
Only then will the majesty of autumn
leave you without concerns.

I like the snow,
and I embrace the cold.
I want to remember every Christmas card
by the time I grow old.
It makes me happy
to feel the flakes floating in the air,
to hear the wind's biting whistle,
and to see that the trees are bare.
It's not a wasteland,
and it's not death.
We must look closely,
to see more than our frozen breath.
A crystal blanket
of fluffy, frozen rain.
Sleigh bells and church bells
ringing again and again.
Frosted evergreens
and rosy cheeks.
Do we dare see its beauty?
Do we dare peek?
Yes, we must,
for it is high time to see
what the rest of the year
hides so carefully.

<u>Spring</u>

A time for renewal,
and rebirth.
It's an annual renaissance,
and it gives.
It gives so much
that we don't always see.
The trees, once barren,
are now budding.
The animals, once hidden,
are awakening.
The sun, once a consolation prize,
is now a jackpot.
When the world opens its doors,
we are there.
But my hope
is that in future,
we won't rush the doors.
We'll walk, not run.
We'll wait our turn.
We'll sip, rather than gulp.
This refreshing time of year
is a marathon,
not a sprint.

They degrade us,
and deplete us.
They cripple us,
and beat us.
We feel helpless and lonely.
We feel used and abused.
We feel.
Boy, do we feel.
But true resilience
isn't measured by how hard we fall.
True resilience
is measured by how boldly we get up.
By how much love is left in our hearts.
By how much stamina is left in our brains.
By how much fight is left in our souls.
That's the measure
of who we really are.

I am who I am
and when I know what that means,
you will, too.
But not before.
Please don't push me
(or pull me, for that matter).
It won't work, and it won't help
settle your own score.
Nurture me, guide me,
but don't forge my path.
I must learn that it's okay
not knowing what's in store.

Innocent lives
(dedicated to Innocent Lives Foundation)


They don't need permission
to smile, to dream, to love.
They are innocent and exuberant,
like angels from above.
But look closely,
for things are not always as they appear.
Behind the light in those pure eyes
can fester an excess of fear.
Can they run and play,
not under a perverted eye?
Can they be online with no worry
of who's watching from the other side?
It is both upsetting and admirable
how quickly they'll bounce back.
It just takes love, trust, and loyalty,
none of which they lack.
But no one is invincible,
especially one so small.
They try, they accept, and they wonder why
until their final fall.
And that is why they need our help.
To the monsters, we must scream and shout.
We must keep the light in those pure eyes
from forever going out.

<u>Better</u>

To be better in future,
we must be better now.
There's no room on earth
for hate.
And yet, it's here.
Imagine,
how much love there could be
if hate went away.
It's always worth it
to be better.

There's power in numbers,
this we all know.
But that doesn't stop us
from feeling alone.
Ask for help,
this we're all told.
And yet, fellow beings
still leave us in the cold.
But we must keep searching
even when we're filled with despair,
because the beauty of hopeful pursuit
is that we will find someone who cares.

Think
outside ourselves more.
Understand
our lives aren't revolving doors.
See
how we can help those who are sore.
Realize
that's what we are here for.

<u>Youth</u>

They say that youth
is wasted on the young.
It seems much too late
for your song to be sung.
But renewal comes
with each trip around the sun.
It's not too late.
It has only just begun.

If you think kindly,
you will act nicely.
If you act nicely,
you will see happiness.
If you see happiness,
you, too, will be happy.
But remember,
it starts with kindness.

<u>Carpe Diem</u>

Be in the moment;
you can't be elsewhere.
At least,
not for real.
Be with your thoughts;
even when they scare you.
After all,
they show what you conceal.
Be more peaceful;
you'll appreciate your life.
And that
is always good to feel.

<u>Peace</u>

If peace is possible,
why don't we have it?
Why do we spend all our time
merely praying for a little bit
of serenity?
All we do is sit
when we should be stopping
the next hit.

What if our mouths
didn't work before our brains?
I'll tell you what.
There'd be much less sadness,
and much less pain.

Just think
about all we take for granted.
Think
about the ones who need us.
Act when necessary.
Speak when necessary.
But for the love of God,
think first.

You are perfect just the way you are.
There will never be another you, near or far.
You are not a burden,
or a bother,
or a ball and chain.
Your purpose is clear; it is precise.
Trust yourself to roll the dice.

<u>Confessions of an anxious mind</u>


It has no face and it has no name,
but when it's here,
it's all there is.
A benign word may seem like slander.
An innocent touch may feel like assault.
And the worst part is
the brain
cannot keep from inflating it.
Let it go.
Move on.
That's what they say.
They have no idea how envied they are,
those who do not
battle their own thoughts
day to day.

Make it make sense.
The clouds in the sky;
the wind in our hair;
the joy;
the hurt;
the laughter;
the tears.
Make it all make sense.
Can we?
Really?
As long as we live
in a biased world,
no.
We cannot.
Because the thing is,
nothing makes sense.
Not to everyone.
Heaven for the spider
is hell for the fly.
Unless we see eye to eye,
or truly walk a mile
in another's shoes,
nothing will make sense.
Ever.

<u>Nothing?</u>

If there's nothing to do,
then there's nothing to see.
Nothing to feel,
or hear,
or taste,
or smell.
As long as we are living,
there cannot be
nothing to do.

Every coin has two faces,
no matter which face you're seeing.
But the problem is the face you see
is the only way you're leaning.
Not a problem? No?
Think again, and take your time.
How can two separate faces
pay tribute to either in their prime?
It's an act, if you will.
An act of balance and precision.
Flip the coin on its side
and bring breadth to your decision.
Only a select few can do it,
but more can learn.
A broader view of both faces
may just simmer the world's burn.
Don't believe me?
Try it, please.
Only then will we maybe
have a little bit of peace.

<u>Feelings</u>

What a blessing and a curse
it is to feel.
Feelings are joyous.
Feelings hurt.
Feelings tell you when you care
and when you don't.
They're gradual
and they're sudden.
They're confusing
and they're clear.
And sometimes
they're not at all that they appear.
To feel is human
and humans must cope,
no matter what a feeling
gives or takes.
No matter how a feeling
makes or breaks.
We must feel
because as we know,
the alternative
is to simply
not.

<u>Pain</u>

I think the reason why pain
is so hard to treat
is because it's never the same.
Aches hurt differently,
and hearts break differently,
because people are different.
Not one person
will ever hurt
in the same way.
And so not one treatment
will ever help
two people.
Pain is what divides us,
but also
what unites us.
It's common ground.
It's something to talk about.
It breeds generosity,
sensitivity,
and compassion.
And quite frankly,
we could do with more of that.
Perhaps
from darkness
there truly does come light.

<u>Hope</u>

How can something
as ubiquitous as hope
be so vastly diverse?
How can it mean
different things
to so many people?
Hope is hope,
isn't it?
Perhaps not.
To some,
it is a driving force.
To others,
it is a state of paralysis.
It is a glass half-full,
but also a glass half-empty.
I suppose hope
will always be different
as long as people are different.
But maybe there's beauty in that.

<u>That horrible day, from a 10-year-old</u>
*(September 11, 2001)*

A world once bright,
once happy,
and once calm,
now filled with darkness,
sadness,
and chaos.
We didn't know
how sheltered we were
before that horrible day.
It took over every conversation.
It occupied every room.
It followed us around
like dense smoke—
the same kind that filled the streets
on that horrible day.
Until then,
we never knew such evil existed
outside of fiction.
Until then,
we were carefree,
and we were innocent.
A child's world, once bright,
once happy,
and once calm
was forever changed
on that horrible day.

There is no outer peace
until there is inner peace.
Personal insecurities
breed fear,
contempt,
and hate.
We cannot truly love our neighbours
until we can truly love ourselves.
We hear someone speaking
in another tongue,
but we should be simply hearing
speaking.
We see a man
loving another man,
but we should be simply seeing
love.
We are far more similar
than we are different.
Until we realize that,
and until we simplify
our own hearts,
we will always be blinded
to the vast potential
that peace has for the world.

Why is kindness a trait
so often overlooked?
I think it's because
it's comfortable.
We don't spend much time
worrying
about comfort.
We worry
about discomfort.
Things like hate,
and violence,
and pain
are given the spotlight.
And so kindness
merely
plays a supporting role.

<u>Memories</u>

If you remember almost everything,
you forget almost nothing.
It's a blessing
and it's a curse.
A blessing because
you always remember the good.
A curse because
you never forget the bad.
But what if we chose to see
the good
as a curse
because it only reminds us of much better times?
And what if we chose to see
the bad
as a blessing
because it reminds us to be grateful at present?
In that case,
what is real
and what is not?
After a certain point,
do any of us truly know?

It's okay to be afraid,
but it's not okay
to stay afraid.
That's why it's the ones
always on the move
who seem to be fearless.
The ones who don't move,
who stay,
are the ones who are stuck in fear.

<u>Allow yourself</u>

If you don't allow yourself
to feel
the way you feel in a moment,
you will lose the feeling.
You can never experience it
in the same way
ever again.
Whether that's good or bad
is up to you,
but you have no choice
if you don't first allow yourself
to feel.

It's the lowest of lows
when you can't find a reason
to care.
It's the harshest of harsh
when you feel there's nobody
there.
It's the coldest of cold
when your mind, not your body,
is bare.
Why bother?
Because where there are lows,
there will come highs.
Because where there is harshness,
things will soften.
Because where it is cold,
warmth is not far behind.

<u>Expectations</u>

The problem with expectations
is that they are seldom met.
The things you want and aim to get
exist only in your head.
And why?
Well,
I think
we spend far too much time
peeking over fences,
spying on our neighbours.
Their end game
might merely be your middle game.
Their unfinished business
might be, to you,
finished.
You are you.
They are they.
No good will come
from you shouldering
their expectations.

<u>Size matters (?)</u>

Most of the time,
I like being small.
But sometimes,
it makes life hard.
When you plead your case,
nobody wants to listen.
When you try to be grown,
nobody wants to see.
This saddens me
because I like being small.
I just don't like
that the world
doesn't listen
or see.

<u>Come together</u>

Different should not mean unequal.
Differing experiences should be shared,
and genuinely understood,
not used as ammunition
or as slander
or misinterpreted
to fit whatever agenda is trending.
We'll never get anywhere
if we don't come together
as one.
And we must come together.
Even if just to consider
that perhaps what makes everybody equal
is the fact that nobody is the same.

Look up
because there's so much to see.
The blue of the sky,
the yellow of the sun,
the green of the treetops,
and how all these colours
blend together
as an infinite mosaic.
Look up
because when you do,
there are no limits.
The sky,
the sun,
and the treetops
can go on together
forever.

Love is a soft-sung whisper

Love is a soft-sung whisper;
a quiet and gentle breeze.
It travels near and far,
seeking a home,
and never, ever will cease.
Through the mountains and trees,
from sea to sea,
it just needs someone to believe.
So let me see and listen,
and let me feel
those blustery murmuring words.
Let me hold them near and dear to my heart,
and the soft-sung whisper be heard.

<u>When my time comes</u>

When I'm gone, I want to know I've been.
I want peace with my time, and
time with my peace.
I want to review my life without remorse.
I want to have taken all the steps
to follow my dreams.
I want to know the energy I spent on my goals
was well worth it, without a doubt.
Without a doubt.
When my time comes, I hope I'll have
the presence of mind to be
without regrets.
When my time comes, I want to use every spare moment
to live and to love as fiercely as I've
lived and loved.
Faced with the choices I've made, the things I've done,
I hope I can be forgiven for some.
Nobody is perfect.
But when my time comes, when I'm gone,
I want people to recall me and smile.
Or, at least chuckle.
I hope they'll say I made my mark on this world.
And I hope I will have done.
Truly.
Because when my time comes,
I just want to know
it's okay.